THE STAMP ACT

At the close of the French and Indian War, Britain gained a large territory in North America and was faced with the added expense of governing it. To help meet the cost of protecting the American colonies, George Grenville, England's Chancellor of the Exchequer, proposed that a stamp tax be levied on various colonial papers and legal documents. But when the British Parliament passed the Stamp Act in 1765, wild controversy broke out in America. As Englishmen, the colonists claimed the right to be taxed only by their own representatives in their own legislatures. They had no representatives in Parliament.

Rioting, demonstrations, and acts of terror prevented the sale of the stamps. American merchants refused to import British goods if the act was enforced. British merchants flooded Parliament with protests. The colonial Stamp Act Congress petitioned against the tax. Finally the Stamp Act was repealed, but not before the American colonists had been aroused to united action and had gained a clearer definition of their fundamental rights.

PRINCIPALS

JOHN ADAMS, a young lawyer of Braintree, Massachusetts.

JAMES OTIS, a radical lawyer of Boston, Massachusetts.

SAMUEL ADAMS, a citizen of Boston and an enemy of the Stamp Act.

THOMAS HUTCHINSON, Lieutenant Governor of Massachusetts.

ANDREW OLIVER, brother-in-law of Hutchinson, and secretary of Massachusetts.

FRANCIS BERNARD, royal governor of Massachusetts.

EBENEZER MACKINTOSH, a Boston shoemaker and a leader in the Stamp Act rioting.

PATRICK HENRY, lawyer, and member of the Virginia House of Burgesses.

GEORGE GRENVILLE, British Chancellor of the Exchequer in 1765, and sponsor of the Stamp Act.

MARQUIS OF ROCKINGHAM, Grenville's successor.

WILLIAM PITT, member of Parliament and friend of the colonies.

COLONEL ISAAC BARRE, member of Parliament and friend of the colonies.

A FOCUS BOOK

The Stamp Act

"Taxation Without Representation Is Tyranny"

by Alice Dickinson

Illustrated with contemporary prints

FRANKLIN WATTS, INC.

575 Lexington Avenue   New York, N.Y. 10022

The authors and publishers of the Focus Books wish to acknowledge the helpful editorial suggestions of Professor Richard B. Morris.

Jacket photo: Library of Congress

Contents

THE STAMP ACT

John Adams

The Remarkable Year

In 1789, at the age of fifty-three, John Adams was to become the first Vice-President of the newly formed United States of America. And later still he would be the nation's second President. But in 1765 he was still a young man — a lawyer, and a citizen of the British colony of Massachusetts.

Already he was interested in politics. His home in Braintree was near Boston — one of the liveliest places in the North American colonies, when it came to politics. John Adams had many acquaintances; he kept his eyes and ears open; he knew what went on behind certain closed doors in Boston; he had formed his own definite opinions about England and her colonies. And he recorded his thoughts and experiences in a diary.

On December 18, 1765, he wrote: "The year 1765 has been the most remarkable year of my life. That enormous engine, fabricated by the British Parliament, for battering down the rights and liberties of America — I mean the Stamp Act — has raised and spread throughout the whole continent a spirit that will be recorded to our honor with all future generations."

The year 1765 had been a restless one in the British colonies of North America. There the people had been faced by a tax put into law by the Stamp Act, passed by the British governing body, the Parliament. The colonists considered the act a threat to their sacred liberties as Englishmen. Their response against it had been strong. They had fought it by every means they could, short of war. And they had even considered that.

In his diary, John Adams went on to describe how those people favoring the stamp tax had been ridiculed and made to feel ashamed and frightened. Everywhere the colonial citizens had talked about their liberties and everywhere there had been heated arguments about the tax.

"Our presses have groaned, our pulpits have thundered, our legislatures have resolved, our towns have voted," wrote Adams. "The Crown officers [those who had supported the Stamp Act] have everywhere trembled, and all their little tools and creatures have been afraid to speak and ashamed to be seen."

Adams chose to mention the protests of the newspapers against the Stamp Act — "our presses have groaned"; the objections of the clergymen — "our pulpits have thundered"; and the actions of the legislatures and the voters. He might also have added: "Our people have rioted and used violence and terror." Never, before the Stamp Act, had there been such a widespread storm of colonial feeling against the British government.

Two Points of View

Other acts of Great Britain had been unpopular, to be sure. This was bound to be true when two groups of people thought as differently as the British and the colonials did.

From the British point of view, the colonies were the property of the mother country and they existed because Great Britain was willing that they should. Their main excuse for being was the economic value they might have for Britain. They furnished raw materials to the mother country, and they were a profitable market for British manufactured goods. In these respects they were important, but they were, after all, only colonies, kept to contribute to the power and wealth of England. Definitely they should be ruled for England's benefit. Most Britishers agreed in this viewpoint.

The colonists thought of themselves in a very different way. Many of the colonies had been begun by private companies, with no particular encouragement from the British government. They had been started on land claimed by Great Britain, but hitherto inhabited only by Indians.

The first settlers had been people who had not been satisfied with the old ways of doing things. They had possessed a little extra dash of curiosity or discontent or desire for adventure. They had left England because a hope or a vision of something better in life had called them across the sea. These people had faced the unknown wilderness and had shaped a new way of living by their own hard efforts. And in turn, the strange new life in a difficult new land had shaped them.

The Mayflower *at anchor off Cape Cod, at the end of her long voyage in 1620.*

Indians welcoming the early New England settlers. (Charles Phelps Cushing)

Three thousand miles of ocean lay between the colonists and home. A ship's voyage across the Atlantic took months. In an emergency, it was impossible to expect help from the homeland. Surrounded by danger as the colonists were, they learned to look out for themselves and they came to have a pride in their ability to do so. They felt independent and self-reliant. Wilderness living gave them a wonderful sense of freedom. Ever so gradually, as the years went by, the colonists began to think of themselves in a new way. As inhabitants of British colonies they considered themselves Englishmen, but Englishmen with a difference. They were American Englishmen, and the well-being of the colonies was their first concern.

Just as the colonials' way of living was different from that in England, so also were their governments. When the new land had first been settled, the colonists had agreed among themselves as to their leaders, and they had governed themselves in general by many of the same laws they had known in England. But not all the old laws made sense in the new country. And the new laws that were needed would have made little sense in England. So, the colonial governments began to take on an American flavor, too.

As time went on, the king and Parliament seemed to matter less and less. They were busy with many troubles at home, and apparently paid little attention to the Americans. For a while the colonists were left more or less to themselves. They thrived on the neglect and thought it only natural that they should manage their affairs in their own way. In fact, they grew to expect this liberty.

The Colonial Governments

In each colony the chief governing group came to be the assembly. Its members were elected by the voters. By 1763, eight of the colonies had royal governors, who represented the king. These governors received instructions from the king and were given the power to veto the laws that were passed by the assemblies. All local laws that the governors approved were sent to

England, where the king's Privy Council made the final decision as to whether these laws were to be allowed.

Each colonial governor had an appointed council, which supported him and was supposed to act as a check on the elected assembly. In many cases, the councilmen were weak and were no match for the assemblies. Then the governors found themselves in a difficult position, particularly in the more independent-minded colonies. Often, if a governor carried out the king's instructions, he was bound to stir up ill will among the colonists. And if he bypassed the king's instructions, he was soon in trouble in England.

Steadfastly the colonists stood by their belief that the assemblies should do most of the governing. There was constant maneuvering between the governors and the councils on the one hand and the assemblies on the other, as the assemblies tested their strength. When they gained the right to appropriate money and oversee its spending, they had a mighty weapon with which to threaten uncooperative governors. Now the assemblies could hold back the pay of officials and they had a certain amount of control over appointments.

Throughout the early years of the eighteenth century the assemblies continued to become more powerful. Most of the laws they passed were allowed to stand, and the colonists enjoyed a great deal of political freedom.

The Navigation Acts

But the colonies were able to thrive, secure against invasion, mainly because English ships were powerful along the ocean trade routes. If England was to remain strong, she must continue to have good trade. Raw materials must be kept flowing into England, and manufactured goods must be sent out at a profit. Only in this way, the English thought, could their country continue to be wealthy and important. The colonists were expected to play their part in this scheme of things.

Other nations in Europe also sought wealth through colonies and trade. France, Spain, and Holland were deadly rivals of England in the struggle for world power. By 1651, Holland had gained a market in the British American colonies. Because of their fine ships and goods and their easy sales terms, the Dutch threatened British trade all over the world.

To encourage English shipping and discourage the trade of rival countries, the British Parliament passed Navigation Acts in 1651, and later, in 1660, 1663, 1673, and 1696. These acts forbade goods to be imported into or exported from the British colonies except in British or colonial ships, with crews made up for the most part of sailors who were British or colonial citizens. Furthermore, ships taking cargoes from Asia or Europe to the British American colonies were required to bring these cargoes first to England and there to pay duties on them. After this, the goods could be shipped across the Atlantic.

Certain natural materials were particularly valuable and were much in demand. Among them were sugar, tobacco, and indigo

A West Indian indigo plantation in the late 1600's. Slaves work at processing the indigo plants, used for dyes. Indigo was a prized British import. (Duterte, Histoire des Antilles, 1667)

for blue dye. All of these grew in one or more of England's colonies in the West Indies or on continental North America. In the Navigation Acts these products and others in demand were listed, or "enumerated." Enumerated goods could be shipped from the colonies only to England and Ireland, then a part of Britain. By making sure that only she received these colonial products, England hoped to become self-sufficient in them.

Throughout the eighteenth century, whenever a product became valuable to England it was added to the enumerated list. Sometimes the colonies lost money through this practice, because they might have got higher prices by trading with other countries than England.

On the whole, the continental American southern colonies fitted into Britain's trading scheme. The crops of the South — tobacco, and later, indigo and rice — were profitable to British merchants. In return for these products the southern planters received manufactured goods from Britain, at whatever prices the merchants cared to charge. The planters had little hard money, as England kept the silver and gold coinage at home. Trading was done on credit. When agricultural prices were low, the southerners bought goods on credit against their next year's crops. But interest rates on this credit were high, and all too often the planters were badly in debt to the English merchants.

To be sure, the Navigation Acts offered some advantages to the colonists. All foreign tobacco was barred from England, so making a protected market for the colonial tobacco growers. Colonial sugar, cotton, and indigo were given tariff protection in England. And bounties, or rewards, were paid to colonists who produced certain of the enumerated raw materials. Yet the colonists resented having prices for their produce fixed by English

A southern colonial tobacco wharf — a drawing from an old map. Slaves roll the huge barrels of tobacco leaves to be loaded onto a waiting English ship, while the plantation owners look on. (New York Public Library)

merchants, and they resented not being allowed to sell their goods wherever they wished, at perhaps higher profits.

The southerners particularly saw themselves as being completely at the mercy of the British traders. Not only were they often in debt, but they also suspected that the price of the goods they received was much too high and that the quality was sometimes inferior.

Any advantage there might have been in the Navigation Acts for the colonists was offset by their discontent and by their feeling that they were somehow being made the victims of the British merchants. Perhaps the colonial point of view was justified, perhaps not. The important thing is that this point of view did exist, and it caused uneasiness in the colonies.

Fish, Lumber, Molasses, and Slaves

The New England colonies were not quite so useful in England's trade scheme as the colonies farther south. The northerners' thin, rock-strewn soil and uncertain climate were not suitable for raising the agricultural products England wanted. Fish and lumber were New England's greatest crops. Except for some timber, and tall white pines for ships' masts, Britain had no use for these products, and the New Englanders were free to take them elsewhere.

They had their own ideas about trade. Along their long coastline were hundreds of little bays and harbors, and their rivers led inland to magnificent forests. This was perfect country for shipbuilding. The Navigation Acts, with their emphasis on British

A view of the colonial port of Boston, a busy shipping center. (Stokes Collection, New York Public Library)

and colonial ships, were a spur to the New England industry. The New Englanders became skilled shipbuilders; they produced some of the best ships in the whole empire.

The men of New England took naturally to the sea. They went north in small boats to fish off the Grand Banks of Newfoundland, and they sailed larger ships on the trade routes. In the West Indies they found a ready market for their fish and lumber.

The West Indies were sugarcane islands. After the plantation owners had refined their cane into sugar, they were left with a by-product: molasses. West Indian molasses was eagerly taken by the New England traders in exchange for their cargoes.

Carried back to the home ports, the molasses was distilled into rum. This liquor, in turn, played its part in another New England trading venture. On the west coast of Africa, rum could

[13]

Negro houses on the coast of Guinea, in Africa. This region was often visited by the slave traders. (Astley, A New and General Collection of Voyages, *1745)*

be exchanged for African tribesmen, who were herded onto ships and brought to the New World as slaves. This was a sickening business, but a profitable one, and the traders closed their eyes to its horrors.

The New Englanders preferred to deal with the plantation owners of the French West Indies, because their molasses was cheaper. But the sugarcane growers in the British West Indies protested against the French trade so vehemently that, in 1733, the British Parliament passed the Molasses Act. This act was aimed at stopping the foreign commerce; it placed a heavy duty on French West Indian molasses imported into the North American colonies.

The New Englanders considered the duty to be so high that

[14]

it would ruin their rum-distilling business. Equally important was the threat to the commerce in their two big natural products, fish and lumber. The British West Indies could not possibly use all the New England cargo, nor could they furnish anywhere near the amount of molasses needed. If trade with the French islands were to be cut off, the northern colonies would lose their most important means of livelihood. In addition to molasses they received a good deal of gold and silver money from their trade. With this they bought necessary goods from England.

At first, the New Englanders raged against the new law. Then they quietly found ways of getting around it. They saw no wrong in smuggling, and quickly became master-hands at it. A little money stealthily passed to a customs official often made him

Slaves work at a sugar refining plant in the West Indies while the plantation owner supervises. Molasses, left over after refining, was bought by New Englanders for making rum. (Duterte, Histoire des Antilles, 1667)

strangely blind to a ship's declaration that listed only half the cargo. Or, for a little money, the officer might charge a lesser duty than that required by law. Besides these methods, there were ways of bringing in cargoes secretly. The New England captains knew all the little creeks and bays along their winding, jigsaw coast. A cargo might be landed in all sorts of places far from customhouses.

Faced with the New Englanders' lack of cooperation, the British customs officers found enforcement of the Molasses Act next to impossible. Finally they gave up any serious attempts at collecting the full duty on foreign molasses.

But while the New Englanders found ways to thwart the Molasses Act, they too resented Great Britain's interference.

The French and Indian War

The difference between the British and colonial points of view was clearly to be seen during the French and Indian War. This war had begun in 1754 with a struggle between France and England for control of the rich lands of the Ohio Valley. If France could build forts and fur-trading posts in this region, they would connect her settlements on the Mississippi River with the rest of New France, which spread north and west of the British colonies. Britain saw that such an outcome would box her colonists into a little strip of land along the coast. Already English settlers were edging westward a few miles at a time. The Ohio Valley offered room for British colonial growth, and it promised great opportunities for trade with the Indians.

The siege of French Louisburg in Canada by the British, in 1758, during the French and Indian War. (Library of Congress)

Much as the colonists would have liked to profit by a British victory over the French in North America, they were less than eager to do their part in winning it. Britain tried requisitioning — calling upon the assembly in each colony to furnish certain numbers of men and amounts of money to help defeat the French. But most of the assemblies were more interested in their own affairs. They were still intent on gaining power over the governors, and they made all sorts of impossible demands in return for their cooperation. Furthermore, there was a great deal of rivalry among the colonies, and each one feared that it might contribute more to the war effort than the others. As a result, many of the colonies hung back at first, eyeing their neighbors and doing almost nothing.

Finally, in 1757, William Pitt came into political power in England. He promised the colonies that they would be repaid their war expenses. When the colonists knew that someone else would be footing the bill, they moved to take an active part in the struggle.

But while colonial soldiers fought the French in the forests, colonial sea captains, especially New Englanders, were smuggling goods to the French West Indies and French Canada. In return, the traders received West Indian goods, which they slipped into their home ports. The provisions shipped by stealth to the enemy almost certainly enabled the French to keep on fighting longer than they might have otherwise, but the colonial traders had their eyes fixed firmly on profits, not on peace or victory.

In 1761, two years before the war ended, a dispute arose between English government officials and the Massachusetts colonists. A British customs officer in Salem, Massachusetts, had asked that a permit, called a writ of assistance, be granted him so that he might make a search for foreign goods he suspected had been smuggled into port and hidden. Writs of this kind had been issued before. They were meant to prevent a customs officer from abusing his power, and they required that he take with him an officer of the court to assist him in gaining entry to any place where he thought smuggled goods might be stored.

The Massachusetts merchants detested search and especially the writs of assistance, which gave blanket permission to a customs officer to enter wherever he wished. The merchants asked two colonial lawyers, James Otis and Oxenbridge Thacher, to plead against the writs in court. Thacher presented his arguments quietly, but Otis burst into a long and impassioned harangue. He claimed that such writs were against the fundamental principles

James Otis, champion of colonial rights. *(Charles Phelps Cushing)*

of law, and he declared that the statute of Parliament making these writs legal in the colonies was unconstitutional.

The writs were finally issued anyway. But Otis had raised a question as to how far the British Parliament could exercise its powers in the colonies. Once raised, the question was not forgotten. Around it a storm of controversy was to rage within a very few years.

A New Plan for America

In 1763, a treaty of peace between France and England marked the settlement of the war. Britain had gained French Canada and the French territory east of the Mississippi River in addition to what is now Florida, and a narrow strip of land stretching westward along the gulf to the Mississippi. She now possessed a vast empire, but along with it she had acquired many problems.

More territory meant, in the first place, that more money must be paid out to govern it. The war had been expensive. In addition to the ordinary military costs, there were the payments promised to the colonies. The mother country was left with an enormous debt. More money must be raised. But already English citizens were reeling under the weight of heavy taxes, and ominous rioting had greeted new levies on cider and beer.

Then there was the problem of the colonies. They had been less than cooperative during the war. Plainly, requisitioning them for money did not work. And might they not become more independent than ever, with the power of the French removed from the North American continent? Now that the empire had grown larger, many British government leaders thought a thorough reorganization of the colonies should be undertaken. Various suggestions were made for bringing them into line.

There was another problem, too. The inland region of North America still needed to be brought under control. The Indians, and also the French settlers, remained a possible threat to the safety of the English colonists.

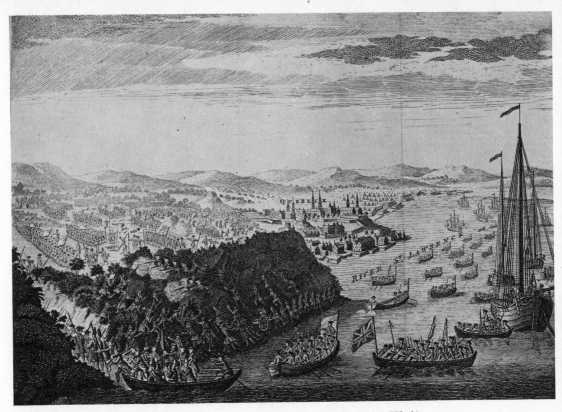

The taking of Quebec by English forces commanded by General Wolfe. This was the decisive battle of the French and Indian War. (Library of Congress)

In 1763, in Pontiac's War, the Indians of the Ohio Valley and the Great Lakes region proved this point by rising in bloody rebellion against British trade arrangements and the entry of British settlers into what the natives considered their territory. In that same year, England, in a proclamation, pledged to honor the claims of the Indians to the lands west of the Appalachian Mountains and to forbid English settlement in those areas unless the natives consented.

Pontiac, leader of the Indian rebellion against the British in 1763. (The Bettmann Archive)

It was decided by the British that an army was needed not only to protect the English colonists but also to defend the rights of the Indians. The British government proposed to send twenty battalions — 10,000 men — to North America, chiefly to be stationed at posts along the frontier and the Great Lakes and in Canada.

This plan would mean even more expense, and the British thought it only fair that the colonies should help bear it. The citizens of England could not be burdened with further taxes, and besides, the troops would be stationed in America for the colonists' protection.

The colonists took a different view. The war years had been prosperous, the colonies were growing, and the Americans were feeling more independent and sure of themselves than ever. Now

[22]

that the French had been defeated, they doubted their need for British protection. They were anxious to spread out into new territory — into the Ohio Valley, among other places.

It was a bad time for England to assert herself. To the colonists, the British seemed intent on curtailing their long-cherished freedom — by keeping them out of the Ohio Valley, by forcing on them an army they did not want, and probably by making them pay for it.

The Sugar Act

In 1763, George Grenville became England's Chancellor of the Exchequer, or its treasurer. On him fell the task of finding a way to solve Britain's money problems, among them paying for the troops to be sent to North America.

Grenville turned his attention to the money already being received from the colonies as customs payments. Considering the amount of trade, the receipts were much too small. Obviously there was smuggling going on, and just as obviously the customs officers were not doing their duty. Some of them did not even work at their posts, but stayed comfortably at home in England while deputies took their places in the colonies. The whole system was inefficient and the cost of running it was much too high.

Now, new regulations ordered all colonial customs officers to their posts. They were required to keep exact accounts of imports and exports. In addition, English warships in American waters were allowed to seize smugglers and receive rewards for so doing.

[23]

George Grenville, British Chancellor of the Exchequer. (The Bettmann Archive)

Everywhere along the coast, customs officers began watching shipping more carefully. Colonial ship captains were required to fill out long, complicated forms for each cargo of goods, even if they were going only a short distance to another part of the colonies. The whole process of law enforcement was made highly favorable to the customs officers and very difficult for suspected culprits.

As it happened, the old Molasses Act of 1733 expired at this time. That act had placed a duty of sixpence a gallon on imported molasses not produced in the British West Indies. Because the duty was so high that it could not be collected, the British Parliament's new Sugar Act of 1764 lowered the levy to threepence a gallon. This was still high, the colonists thought, but this time the British clearly intended to collect the money. In the same act, duties on some other imports were raised, and foreign rum and French wines were banned entirely as imports into the colonies.

By 1764, the colonies were suffering a postwar depression, and times were hard. The colonial importers protested the trade laws because of their bad effect on business.

[24]

But a few colonists saw something even more threatening about the Sugar Act. The Navigation Acts, while they had imposed duties on some imports, had been passed primarily to regulate trade, not to raise money. For the most part, the colonies, much as they resented the acts, had felt that Britain was within her rights in making laws to adjust colonial commerce.

The Sugar Act, however, made no pretense at being a trade-regulating act. It definitely stated that its purpose was to raise revenue, or money, in America "for defraying the expenses of defending, protecting, and securing the same."

In Massachusetts, Samuel Adams—a radical and a resident of Boston — Oxenbridge Thacher, Thomas Hutchinson, and some other men were quick to see that in raising revenue the British Parliament was imposing a tax on the colonies.

To make things worse, Grenville had realized that the income from the Sugar Act would not pay much toward keeping troops in America. At the time he introduced the act into Parliament he had also proposed a resolution stating that it might be necessary to raise so-called stamp duties — more taxes — in America. Parliament had approved the resolution, but Grenville had postponed action on it for the time being.

The American colonists had always clung jealously to their rights as Englishmen, which had been guaranteed to them in the charters granted the colonies by the British government. One of the most precious of these rights was that of being taxed only by their own representatives in their own elected governing assemblies.

There were no colonial representatives in the British Parliament. Had Parliament, then, the power to tax the colonists? The answer, as Samuel Adams and his friends saw it, was a resounding

Samuel Adams, one of the chief agitators against taxes imposed on the colonists by Britain. (Metropolitan Museum of Art)

No. In May, 1764, a committee made up of Adams and a few others wrote instructions to the Boston representatives in the Massachusetts assembly. They asked that the representatives protest the Sugar Act and the proposed stamp duties not only because of the heavy burden on the colonists, but also because of the threat to their rights.

"These unexpected proceedings," wrote Samuel Adams, "may be preparatory to new taxations upon us; for if our trade may be taxed, why not our lands? Why not the produce of our lands and everything we possess or make use of? This . . . annihilates our charter right to govern and tax ourselves. It strikes at our British privileges, which as we have never forfeited them, we hold in common with our fellow subjects who are natives of Britain. If

[26]

taxes are laid upon us in any shape without our having a legal representation where they are laid, are we not reduced from the character of free subjects to the miserable state of tributary slaves?"

James Otis' question about the power of Parliament had been raised again. In October, the Massachusetts assembly adopted a protest to the English government about taxation, although the council, at the insistence of Lieutenant Governor Thomas Hutchinson, toned it down somewhat. Other colonies also protested, some in outspoken terms, that they were being taxed by a governing body in which they had no representation.

In Britain, these protests were received coldly. The colonists' denial of the right of Parliament to tax them had an effect just the opposite of that intended. Many British people saw such talk as a threat that the colonists were indeed becoming too independent in their thinking. Government officials became more determined than ever to tax them.

The Stamp Act

In Grenville's opinion, a stamp duty was the fairest tax that could be raised in the colonies. He did not think that the financial burden would be heavy on any one group of people, but would instead be spread among all the citizens. Stamp taxes had worked well in England.

In the colonies, a tax, indicated by a stamp, would be put on a great variety of legal and commercial papers: newspapers, pamphlets, almanacs, wills, college diplomas, ships' bills of lading

*Stamp, embossed on paper, for a shilling tax.
(Massachusetts Historical Society)*

and customhouse papers, all sorts of contracts — even on playing cards. The stamps on documents would be embossed on paper. This embossed paper would be furnished by the British Board of Stamp Commissioners and sold at prices depending on the amount of the tax. The price would vary for different kinds of documents, and for some it would be quite high. No document would be legal unless it bore a stamp.

In 1764, Grenville had delayed passing the stamp tax for a year, partly because he feared that acting too quickly would arouse the colonists' anger. By postponing the tax, he hoped that the colonies would become used to the idea and would agree to it of their own will. Then too, it was necessary to gather information from America in order to draw up the tax plan. At the time he had first proposed the stamp duty, Grenville stated that if the colonies could think of a better tax method, he would be glad to consider it.

To look out for its interests, each colony had an agent in

[28]

London. Grenville spoke to these agents, saying that he wished to tax the colonies according to the plan most acceptable to them. But he warned that if no satisfactory tax proposal came from them, he would ask Parliament to pass a stamp tax. He hoped, moreover, that the colonists would agree with his ideas.

The colonists were in no mood to welcome a tax plan proposed by Britain. There was the all-important question of their rights as Englishmen, and there were other things. Having their trade regulated by England had been bad enough before, but now the Sugar Act made things worse.

The hard money available in the North American colonies had come mostly from the foreign West Indian trade. Now the Sugar Act enforced more strictly the paying of duties on foreign molasses, and Britain had forbidden the use of paper money. The colonists were at a loss to see how they could pay a tax, even if one were demanded. All the resentments that had been accumulating over the years began to come to a boil.

But Grenville seemed not to take the protests of the colonists seriously, and apparently he did not think that they would come up with an alternative plan. His assistants set about gathering information on what the taxable items in the colonies were, and began drawing up a stamp act.

The colonial agents were receiving letters from home and they had at least some idea of what might be brewing in America. At one point they suggested a system of requisitioning the colonies for money. But Grenville knew how badly this had worked during the French and Indian War. There was no reason to think it would work better now.

On February 2, 1765, four days before the stamp tax plan was laid before Parliament for the first time, the colonial agents

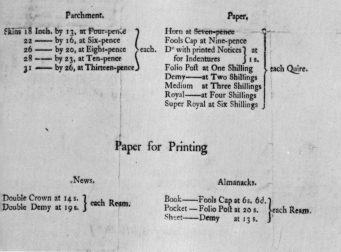

*Price list from the London Stamp
Office, 1765, listing American
colonial taxes to be paid on various kinds and sizes of paper.
(New York Public Library —
Green, Ten Facsimile Reproduc-
tions)*

met with Grenville. They told him of the colonial feeling and
proposed that if a tax must be laid on America, the colonial assemblies should be allowed to levy it.

Grenville argued for his plan, but the agents replied that if
the assemblies raised the money, the colonists would at least feel
it was their own act, and moreover their own officers could best
collect the tax.

Grenville then asked if the agents had decided how much
money each colony should contribute. Upon hearing that they

[30]

had not, he gave an answer that was pure hypocrisy. He replied that no one in England had the information for estimating the amounts each colony should pay, and moreover, there was no certainty that the colonists would contribute the money. He ended by saying that he was pledged to lay the Stamp Act before Parliament.

But it was the British Board of Trade's job to furnish estimates of a colonial tax — not the colonial agents'. The agents had no way of getting the necessary information. Apparently, Grenville was not anxious to consider seriously colonial ideas on taxation. He had already made up his mind on a stamp tax.

When the act was debated in Parliament, there was some opinion against it, but not a great deal. The Stamp Act was finally passed, and became law on March 22, 1765. It put taxes on a wide range of papers and documents, and was to become effective on November 1, 1765. The money raised was to go toward paying for troops in the colonies.

Opposition in the Colonies

The protests in America were continuing. With colonial trade already in the doldrums, the colonists asked each other how they could pay the tax.

But more than money was worrying them. What were the British planning for the future? they wondered. If Parliament could tax the colonies once, it could do it again and again. In time, the assemblies would lose control of colonial finances, and the

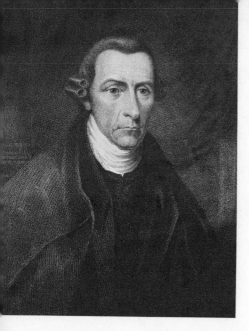

Patrick Henry, of Virginia. (Charles Phelps Cushing)

governors would no longer be dependent on the people's will. What would happen then to the liberties the colonists had guarded so carefully over the years? And what about their English right to be taxed only by their own representatives?

It was a young backcountry lawyer, Patrick Henry of Virginia, who finally put the feeling of the people into words that echoed and reechoed throughout the colonies. On May 29, 1765, he introduced a set of resolutions into the Virginia assembly, the House of Burgesses. These resolutions stated that by charter the colonists of Virginia had been granted all the rights and liberties of Englishmen; that taxation by the people themselves or by their representatives was one of the English liberties; and that the general assembly of Virginia had the sole right to lay taxes on the inhabitants of that colony. It further stated that any attempt to give such power to persons other than the assembly would tend to destroy British as well as American freedoms.

Apparently Henry had considered two more resolutions that were much stronger than the ones he actually introduced into the House of Burgesses. In newspapers throughout the colonies these additional resolves were reported. They stated that the Virginians were not bound to obey any taxation laws except their own and that anyone who declared that outside persons had the power to tax Virginians should be considered an enemy of the colony.

The newspaper accounts led citizens in the other colonies to believe that the Virginians had decided to resist the Stamp Act. Now, more than ever, the people discussed their rights, and more than ever the outcry against the taxes grew. Since the colonies did not send representatives to the British Parliament, the colonists argued, that body had no power to lay taxes on them.

The Resistance Grows

Even before news of Patrick Henry's resolutions had reached the other colonies, plans were being made to protest the Stamp Act in an orderly way. On June 8, 1765, the Massachusetts assembly voted to ask all the colonial assemblies to send representatives to a congress in New York in October. This congress would draw up a petition to George III, king of England, asking relief not only from the Stamp Act, but also from the trade acts and duties.

In the meantime, the colonial newspapers were raging against the act, and patriot groups were secretly planning direct action. The report of Patrick Henry's resolutions added fuel to the flames.

Grenville had tried to make the Stamp Act more agreeable

Edes and Gill, publishers of the Boston Gazette, *were staunch Sons of Liberty and opponents of the Stamp Act. On the first page of their paper for October 7, 1765, they published this "emblem of the effects of the fatal stamp." (New York Public Library)*

to the colonists by appointing colonial citizens as stamp distributors to take charge of the stamped paper and sell it. The positions paid fairly good salaries, and he thought that Americans would be pleased to accept them. Even Benjamin Franklin, leading colonial agent in London, who had fought the Stamp Act, thought that once the act was passed, the colonies would go along with it, though unwillingly. He had misjudged colonial opinion so far as to recommend a friend as a distributor.

Now word began to leak out as to who the distributors in each colony would be. Feeling against these men ran high. They were regarded as villains and traitors. The stamp distributors were to become the first victims of the patriot groups.

Boston, whose citizens were always touchy where their rights were concerned, led the way. The town had a ready-made patriots' organization in the Caucus Club, which had operated for some years as a political machine that directed elections from behind the scenes. In February, 1764, John Adams made this entry in his diary: "This day [I] learned that the Caucus Club meets, at certain times, in the garret of Tom Dawes, the Adjutant of the

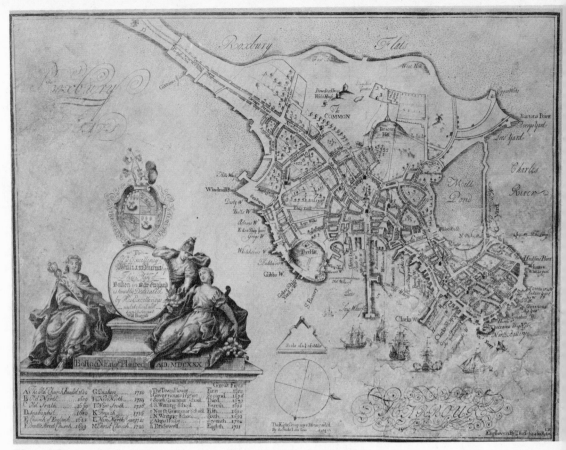

Plan of Boston in the 1700's. (Metropolitan Museum of Art)

Boston Regiment. He has a large house, and he has a movable partition in his garret which he takes down, and the whole club meets in one room. There they smoke tobacco till you cannot see from one end of the garret to the other. There they drink flip, I suppose, and there they choose a moderator, who puts questions to the vote regularly; and selectmen, assessors, wardens, fire-wards, and representatives are regularly chosen before they are chosen in the town. . . . They send committees to wait on the merchants club and to propose and join in the choice of men and measures."

The Caucus Club was definitely a power in Boston. From this group, nine men, known as the Loyall Nine, became the leaders of the resistance to the Stamp Act. They kept their names secret, though they were known to Samuel Adams and to some others, among them John Adams, who paid the nine a visit in their headquarters. They met in a room on the second floor of a distillery. On John Adams' visit he found no intrigue, but had a pleasant social time with "punch, wine, pipes and tobacco, biscuit and cheese."

In private, though, this room was the nerve center of the Boston resistance movement. From this spot, word went out whenever a mob was to be raised or mischief was to be done against Stamp Act sympathizers.

It had been reported that Andrew Oliver, secretary of Massachusetts, was to be appointed stamp distributor for the province. Aroused by the Virginia resolutions, the Loyall Nine decided to frighten him into resigning the post.

On the morning of August 14, 1765, Oliver's effigy, a dressed-up dummy made to look like him, was found hanging from a tree in the center of Boston. Some members of the governor's council thought the hanging was only harmless sport, but Lieutenant Governor Hutchinson and Governor Francis Bernard feared it was a serious matter. Hutchinson ordered the sheriff and his officers to take the effigy down, and Bernard called the council to meet that afternoon to decide what to do in case the sheriff was prevented from carrying out his duty. Before the council could come together, the law officer returned with word that he could

[36]

One of the many cartoons published in Britain at the time of the Stamp Act. While King George III pleads with his treasurer for money, the stamp collector tries to snatch a bag of gold from the American colonists. (British Museum)

not remove the effigy without danger to his life from the crowd gathered around the tree.

That afternoon the council debated what action to take. As darkness fell a large mob came by, bearing the effigy and shouting. They marched to a new building that Oliver had just put up, and quickly pulled it to the ground. They they went to Oliver's home, beheaded the effigy, and broke all the house windows facing the street.

After the effigy had been burned on Fort Hill, some of the more reputable members of the crowd went home. But a large number returned to Oliver's house. Oliver and his family had been

[37]

persuaded to leave, while a few of his friends remained behind to protect the property. When the mob found the street doors barricaded, they tore down a fence, entered the garden, and broke all the windows and doors facing it. Oliver's friends escaped as the mob rushed into the building, looking for him and screaming that they would kill him. When they could not find him they began tearing apart the house and its furniture.

At eleven o'clock, Lieutenant Governor Hutchinson and the sheriff came, in an attempt to disperse the crowd. They were pelted with stones, and barely escaped serious injury before they fled. Then Governor Bernard directed the colonel of the militia to have one of his drummers beat an alarm to assemble the militiamen. But the colonel replied that it would do no good, as the drummer would be knocked down and his drum broken — and besides, all the drummers of the regiment were probably in the mob. Finally the members of the crowd went home of their own will.

The next morning, Oliver, under threat, was forced to resign his post as stamp distributor, although actually he had not yet received a commission for the job.

One of the leaders of the mob had been Ebenezer Mackintosh, a shoemaker who lived in the South End and was the head of a gang that regularly fought a rival group in the North End. The Loyall Nine could see the advantages of having a man like Mackintosh to do their bidding, and they persuaded him to transfer his energies from street fighting to a patriotic cause. From that time on, Mackintosh was the leader of the rioting.

After the attack on Oliver's house, Boston was fairly quiet until August 26. On that day a rumor started that trouble was about to break out again. Toward evening a bonfire was lighted in front of the Town House, horns and whistles were sounded, and a large crowd assembled, shouting, "Liberty and property" — the signal that a house was to be plundered. Still shouting, the crowd went first to the home of the marshal of the admiralty court, but there they were bought off with a barrel of punch. After a pleasant period of drinking they went on to the house of the register of the same court. Here they took all the legal books and papers and made a bonfire of them. Growing ever more enthusiastic about their evening's work, they next visited the home of the controller of customs, broke in, destroyed everything of value, and carried off all the money they could find.

But the main event of the evening was yet to come. This was a visit to the home of Lieutenant Governor Thomas Hutchinson. He had been against the Stamp Act when it was first proposed, and he still was not in favor of it. But he had argued for a weakening of the assembly's protest to the king against it. Besides that,

Thomas Hutchinson, Lieutenant Governor of Boston in 1765. (The Bettmann Archive)

he was Oliver's brother-in-law, and the two men together held many of the best government jobs in the province. Hutchinson was a superior public servant, but he was a cool and distant man who was envied and was unpopular. Now Mackintosh led the crowd against him.

Hutchinson, forewarned, had sent his family away, but had decided to stay in his house and face the mob. His eldest daughter, however, when she had gone a little way, returned and refused to leave unless he went with her. He finally agreed — a fortunate thing as, if he had remained, he might well have lost his life. When the visitors arrived they proceeded systematically to wreck the interior of the building. Everything movable was destroyed except objects of value — money, silverware, jewelry, and other such things — which were carried off. Perhaps the greatest loss was a valuable collection of manuscripts and original documents having to do with the history of the colony. Many of these were scattered and destroyed — lost forever.

The house was imposing and substantial, and the mob worked until dawn, trying to tear down its outer walls, but with little success. The next morning the streets were littered with some of the valuables that had been dropped as they were taken away. It had been the wildest night Boston had known in many years.

While quite a few Bostonians had applauded the wrecking of Oliver's home, there was a general feeling of shock about the attack on Hutchinson. Most people saw him as an innocent victim. They felt that resistance to the Stamp Act was turning into a matter of looting and personal revenge. It became known that the mob was making a list of the houses to be attacked next — fifteen in all. Some of the wealthier enemies of the Stamp Act began to fear for their own property.

Governor Bernard called on the militia to assemble and guard the town. This time it obeyed, and order was once more established. Ebenezer Mackintosh had been arrested for his part in the Hutchinson affair. But perhaps he knew too much about the men who had planned the rioting, and if he had to appear in court that knowledge might become public. When threats were made that none of the militia would stand guard in the town if he were held, Ebenezer Mackintosh walked out of jail a free man. No one was ever punished for the terrible damage done to Hutchinson's home.

"We do every thing in order to keep this and the first affair private, and are not a little pleased to hear that Mackintosh has the credit for the whole affair," said one of the Loyall Nine in speaking of the destruction to Hutchinson's and Oliver's property.

From then on, Mackintosh kept his mob under better control, and Boston quieted down somewhat. In September, when the stamped paper arrived from England, Governor Bernard prevented another crisis by storing it in Castle William, the British fort in the harbor.

But news of the trouble had spread throughout the colonies, and soon other patriotic groups were following Boston's example in forcing the resignation of the stamp distributors. These action groups, in Boston and elsewhere, adopted the name "Sons of Liberty." In every colony they were in the forefront of the resistance to the Stamp Act. Much of the agitation took the form of mob violence — rioting, destruction of property, and attacks on individuals. The mobs were made up of laborers, shopkeepers, and mechanics, but apparently their activities were planned and directed by professional and well-to-do people such as lawyers and merchants.

In colony after colony, the Sons of Liberty wrecked the

houses of the stamp distributors, threatened their lives, chased them out of town, and forced them to resign in terror. By November 1, 1765, there were no colonial distributors to take charge of the stamps.

Quieter Resistance

Quieter and more dignified ways of protesting the Stamp Act were also being tried. On October 7, 1765, the Stamp Act Congress met in New York. Delegates were present from nine colonies — Massachusetts, Connecticut, Rhode Island, New York, New Jersey, Pennsylvania, Delaware, Maryland, and South Carolina. New Hampshire, North Carolina, Georgia, and Virginia sent no representatives, and the delegates from South Carolina, Connecticut, and New York came without any authority from their colonies to sign a petition.

Some of the outstanding men of America attended. Among them were a number of hotheaded radicals, but the more conservative members soon gained control of the meeting. These men argued for making clear the rights and privileges of the colonies while at the same time admitting the authority of the king and Parliament.

The final declaration of the congress stated the colonists' allegiance to the British Crown and acknowledged Parliament's authority. But it asserted the colonists' right to be taxed only by their own representatives. It argued that the stamp duties were damaging to the liberties of the colonists, and stated that these

George III, King of England at the time of the Stamp Act. (Charles Phelps Cushing)

duties and others were burdensome and impossible to pay because there was so little hard money in America. The declaration also stated that because the colonists were forced to trade with England at a profit to British merchants, a great deal of money was already being contributed to the mother country. There was a reminder, too, that the trade restrictions might soon make it impossible for the colonists to buy British goods. For all these reasons the colonists petitioned the repeal of the Stamp Act and the trade acts.

The work of the congress was eventually approved by every colony but Virginia, whose royal governor had prevented its assembly from meeting.

The petition was sent off to England while the Sons of Liberty worked out another persuader to convince the British to repeal the Stamp Act. This next move was aimed directly at trade with Britain. If the colonial merchants were to stop importing

British goods, powerful pressure would be put on the English merchants to oppose the Stamp Act. On October 31, 1765, the day before the act was to go into effect, a meeting of New York merchants agreed not to buy goods from Britain until the Stamp Act was repealed. Soon merchants in Philadelphia and the New England ports had entered into similar agreements.

November Comes

The first of November came, when the Stamp Act was presumably in force. The colonists greeted the day with muffled church bells, and flags flying at half-mast. Some Americans even wore mourning. In New York there was a violent riot that almost resulted in serious bloodshed between the Sons of Liberty and British troops.

Now arose the question of what to do about ships' papers, legal documents, and all the other papers that should bear a stamp. In other colonies besides Massachusetts the stamped paper had arrived, but the Sons of Liberty had staged riots and put up posters threatening the persons and property of anyone who dared use it. British authorities in America, all too aware that the paper would make a splendid bonfire, kept it in safely guarded places. The Sons of Liberty were demanding that all business go on as usual, without the stamps.

Many ships had already sailed from harbor or had obtained papers dated before November 1. For these ships the question of stamps would not arise for a while. But soon cargoes were piling

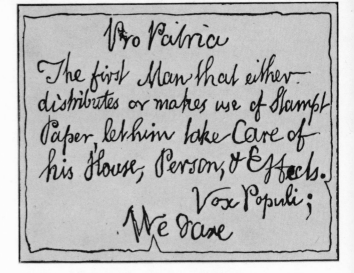
up on the docks, and colonial shipowners were beginning to ask that the customs officers clear ships — make out papers allowing them to sail.

As it happened, the stamped paper for customs clearances had not arrived in Virginia. Because of this, the head of customs for that province authorized his officers to let ships sail with unstamped papers. Soon merchants and shipowners in the other colonies were pointing out that while stamped paper may have arrived in their ports, there was no one to distribute it, and so it was unavailable. They asked that they be allowed the same clearances as in Vir-

The New York Mercury *for November 18, 1765, was published without stamps, but with the explanation that there were no stamps to be had. (New York Public Library)*

-[No *Stamped Paper* to be had.]

From the PUBLIC LEDGER, August 16.

A Dialogue between a North-American and a Courtier.

North-American.

YOU remember that at our last meeting, we agreed upon this day candidly to enquire into the justice as well as policy of Great-Britain, in taxing the North-Americans: and as this is a matter of the greatest importance to both countries, I shall with pleasure hear you endeavour to defend the measures that have been taken to the utmost of my power, I mean as far as is consistent with truth or right reason; but if I should differ with you in opinion, I hope you will bear me with the same candor that I shall you.

Courtier.

Upon these principles, Sir, I join issue; and first, as to the justice or right of Taxing. This I think we are vested with, from your being the subjects of the Crown of England, as well as in consideration of the protection and repeated succours you have received from this nation, to which you owe your origin and which so often has de-

LONDON, August 29.

His Excellency the Earl of Hertford, Lord Lieutenant of Ireland, has appointed the Hon. Col. Cuninghaim, and Capt. Fleming, to be his Aids de Camp.

Very large Orders from Spain are come over for the purchase of corn, so great a scarcity of which has not been known there for many years.

A Letter from on board the Hardwicke Indiaman, in St. Jago road, capital of the Cape de Verd Islands, dated May 16, mentions, that she touched there the 8th of that Month for Water, (having had a very good passage) where she found the Hector and True Briton. The Royal Charlotte came in there for water a few days after.

A Ship, John Hop, Master, from Bordeaux bound to Hamburgh, was boarded in the British Channel by pirates, under English Colours, and robbed of two Casks indigo, and a chest of wine, with some

and not chiming in with the oppressive Measures of those in Power, having had many broad Hints and Overtures, to bring them over for that Purpose. Which they rejected with Disdain. I should be very sorry to find your Paper under so much undue Influence, as to omit inserting Things of so great Consequence to the Peace, Happiness, and Tranquility of the Public in general. I cannot in Justice to these Gentlemen's Characters, read your Papers, without making some Reply to so great a Falsity.

I am, Sir, *Your obedient Servant,*
A Citizen of Montreal.

N. B. For Conveniency, we have new Comission of the Peace every Quarter Sessions; suppose it is so in the other Colonies.

St. Jago, (Jamaica) August 14.

Extract of the Assembly of the 16th August.

A Message from his Excellency by the Provost Marshal, commanding in his Majesty's Name, the immediate Attendance of the House in the Council Chamber; Mr. Speaker and the whole House attending his Excellency, his Excellency addressed the Speaker in the Words fol-

ginia. By the middle of December, colonial ships were sailing normally, with unstamped papers.

Many newspapers had continued to come out without stamps, and many other kinds of papers such as diplomas and wills were being written on unstamped paper. The courts were more cautious about conducting business without stamps, but by March many of them had opened and were proceeding in the old way.

As far as the colonies were concerned, the Stamp Act might almost not have been passed, except for some small inconveniences and the disturbances and anxiety it caused. No one knew what the English authorities might do, now that they were faced with the colonists' rebellion against using stamped paper.

If Great Britain should decide to use her army to enforce the Stamp Act, the Sons of Liberty were determined to resist. All during the winter of 1765–66 they met and talked strategy. The separate colonies, which until recently had felt closer to England than to each other, were discovering the strength that lies in unity. Plans were being made to band together if Great Britain should use her military might.

In December, two delegates from the New York Sons of Liberty met with some of the Connecticut group. They talked of sending armed men to aid each other's colonies in a crisis. According to a letter received by John Adams, "The worthy Sons of Liberty in New York and Connecticut . . . have signified their determination to march with all dispatch at their own costs and expenses, on the first proper notice, with their whole force (if required) to the relief of those who shall or may be in danger from the Stamp Act or its abettors, and to keep a watchful eye over all those who, from the nature of their offices, vocations, or dispositions, may be the most likely to introduce the use of stamped

With Grief and Anger mixt, *Diploma* now,
Starts from his Seat and knits his manly Brow.
" Muſt I be ſt--pt (ſays he) and baſely die
Under th' oppreſſive Hand of Tyr---y ?
When I have bent my utmoſt Skill and Knowledge
To ſerve the Cauſe of Learning and the College ?
Will all the Men of Science me neglect,
When I do them ſo carefully protect
From thoſe Indignities which vulgar Men
Would, otherwiſe, be bold to caſt on them ?
When I their Education tell around,
And cauſe their Reputation to abound,
Shall I no Privilege hereby obtain,
But cry, to thoſe I've ſerv'd, for Help in vain ?"
   The *Licence Paper* next, with ruddy Face,
No longer can, in Silence, keep his Place ;
But cries (with Spirits high, and Blood inflam'd)
" Think I'll be ſt--pt ! I'll ſooner much be d---d !
For Ages paſt I've fill'd the generous Bowl,
And pour'd ſeraphick Pleaſures on the Soul
Of old and young, the Stateſman and the Prieſt,
And lull'd their troubled Minds to quiet reſt.
I've rais'd their drooping Spirits when ſunk low,
And diſſipated all their Grief and Woe.
But, with unquenched Thirſt, they all ſhall pine,
If they won't pity ſuch a Caſe as mine."
   The *Paper* which retails the weekly News,
Seems alſo bent the St--p-A-t to refuſe ;
And cries, " Oh ! hard indeed my Fate muſt be, ⎫
If from the D---l's Foot I mayn't be free, ⎬
To bear the *D---l's Tail's* † enough for me. ⎭

† *A vulgar Name for the large Handle of a Printing Preſs.*

Even books protested the Stamp Act. A page from A New Collection of Verses Applied to the First of November, A.D. 1765. *This poem brings various pieces of paper — diplomas, licenses, wills, newspapers — to life as people and lets them speak of their grief at being stamped. The words "stamp" and "Stamp Act" are never spelled out, but are partly filled in with hyphens. (New York Public Library)*

paper, to the total subversion of the British constitution and American liberty."

Other delegates were enlisting help in Boston. For the next three months, letters went back and forth and there was a flurry of visits and secret meetings as the Sons of Liberty laid their plans to help one another. Had Britain decided to use her army to enforce the Stamp Act, there would certainly have been bloodshed and a determined fight by the colonists.

The Stamp Act Is Repealed

The colonial governors were writing long, pessimistic reports to England about the colonists' resistance to the act. Perhaps more importantly, back in Britain the government was facing resistance from another group. The English merchants and manufacturers, who had never really favored the act, were suffering from the lack of trade brought on by the colonial nonimportation agreements. And they were not suffering in silence. Their complaints, long and loud, could be heard the length and breadth of the land. The heartbeat of British trade was the commerce with the North American colonies. Now it was almost stilled. Business was bad, the merchants faced ruin, and if bankruptcy came, the whole of England would feel its effects.

Like the merchants overseas in America, the British merchants banded together to take action. They appointed a committee to organize the English enemies of the Stamp Act so that they could make known their feelings to Parliament. This committee composed a letter that was sent to thirty of the large shipping and manufacturing towns of England. It asked merchants and manufacturers to protest. As a result, members of Parliament were overwhelmed with a flood of petitions from British traders everywhere in the land. They all demanded one thing: the repeal of the Stamp Act. The British businessmen cared little about the right of the colonies to tax themselves, and they made little mention of it. Their petitions emphasized the financial trouble that England would surely be in if trade with the colonies was not resumed.

In July, 1765, Grenville, after quarreling with the king, had been replaced by the Marquis of Rockingham. By late autumn, word of the American resistance to the Stamp Act was reaching England, and the English merchants were demanding the act's repeal. But, on the other hand, a powerful group in Parliament did not want to give in to the colonies, because they feared that the Stamp Act rioting might be a first move toward colonial independence. Rockingham was caught between two opposing groups — those who favored repeal and those who did not. He put off doing anything until January, 1766. By that time, pressures against the Stamp Act were so strong that Parliament was forced to take action. The question was, What action should it take?

William Pitt, who had been head of government during the French and Indian War and was still a leader in British politics, spoke against taxing the colonies, but upheld Britain's authority to make laws governing them.

"It is my opinion," he said, "that this kingdom has no right to lay a tax upon the colonies. At the same time, I assert the authority of this kingdom over the colonies, to be sovereign and supreme in every circumstance of government and legislation whatsoever. They are the subjects of this kingdom, equally entitled with our-

William Pitt, British leader who opposed the Stamp Act.

selves to all the natural rights of mankind and the peculiar privileges of Englishmen. . . . Taxation is no part of the governing or legislative power. The taxes are a voluntary gift and grant of the Commons [people] alone.

"The Commons of America, represented in their several assemblies, have ever been in possession of the exercise of this, their constitutional right, of giving and granting their own money. They would have been slaves if they had not enjoyed it. At the same time, this kingdom, as the supreme governing and legislative power, has always bound the colonies by her laws, by her regulations, and restrictions in trade, in navigation, in manufactures, in every thing except that of taking their money out of their pockets without their consent.

"Here I would draw the line."

Grenville, still a member of Parliament, replied that the

power to tax was a part of the whole of Britain's power over her colonies.

"That this kingdom has the sovereign, the supreme legislative power over America is granted," he said. "It cannot be denied; and taxation is a part of that sovereign power. It is one branch of legislation. It is, it has been, exercised over those who are not, who were never, represented. . . . It was exercised over the palatinate of Chester, and the bishopric of Durham, before they sent representatives to Parliament."

At this time, there were parts of England that did not actually elect representatives to Parliament. But those who were elected were considered to be representatives of all Englishmen. Some members of Parliament applied the same principle to the colonists, saying that though they did not send representatives, they were "virtually" represented in Parliament, just as the people who lived in England were.

When it came to taxes, however, there was a difference between the colonists and the residents of England. Whatever taxes the members of Parliament voted to be levied in England, they themselves would have to pay, along with other Englishmen. When members of Parliament voted colonial taxes, however, they were voting something they did not have to pay, and they were making their own tax burden lighter. The colonists were well aware of this difference and the dangers in it, and so was William Pitt.

"I rejoice that America has resisted," he said.

Pitt pointed out the great profits that came to Great Britain from trade with the American colonies. There was a clear distinction between taxes levied for the purpose of raising revenue, and duties imposed for the regulation of trade, he said.

Benjamin Franklin, a colonial agent in London at the time of the Stamp
Act. (Metropolitan Museum of Art)

Somehow, the belief arose among many members of Parliament that the Americans were objecting only to "internal" taxes — taxes levied on them within their colonies — and were not objecting to "external" taxes — taxes on their outside trade. Benjamin Franklin, chief agent for the colonies, testified in Parliament. He was eager to get the Stamp Act repealed, and he did not clear up the confusion between internal and external taxes. He was asked if it was true that the colonists felt that there was no difference between the two kinds of taxes and that neither should be levied on them. He managed to give the impression that the Americans were protesting only against internal taxes. Though this was not strictly the case, it was a comforting idea to the members of Parliament and may have helped reconcile them to the step that had to be taken.

As a solution to the Stamp Act problem, William Pitt suggested that the act be repealed, but that Parliament at the same time declare the authority of England over the colonies. This solution should be agreeable to both sides in Parliament's dispute.

Rockingham's ministry took the hint from William Pitt. The Rockingham cabinet decided upon repeal of the Stamp Act, and proposed a resolution that declared that "Parliament had, hath, and of right ought to have, full power and authority to make laws and statutes of sufficient force and validity to bind the colonies and people of America, subjects of the Crown of Great Britain, in all cases whatsoever."

But what did "in all cases whatsoever" mean? Did it include the power of Parliament to pass colonial tax laws?

Colonel Isaac Barré, who had fought in the colonies during the French and Indian War and who understood their viewpoint, moved that the phrase "in all cases whatsoever" should be left out

[53]

Colonel Isaac Barré, member of Parliament, who fought to repeal the Stamp Act.

of the declaration. He was seconded in this motion by William Pitt. They based their arguments on taxation in the colonies. Taxation could not be undertaken by Parliament, they claimed, because the colonists were not represented in that body and it was highly impractical for them to send representatives from overseas. Therefore, "in all cases whatsoever" was not a fitting phrase.

When the motion of Barré and Pitt to strike out the phrase was defeated, Parliament naturally concluded that "in all cases whatsoever" referred to taxation too, because that was what Barré and Pitt had talked about.

Now that this matter was decided, the action for repeal went forward. Members of Parliament pointed out how the trade interests of Britain were suffering, and how difficult, if not impossible, the Stamp Act would be to enforce in America. In March,

1766, repeal and the Declaratory Act were finally approved by the king. It was stated that continuing the Stamp Act would cause many inconveniences and might have results harmful to the commercial interests of the kingdom. The Declaratory Act affirmed Parliament's power and authority to make laws binding the colonies in all cases whatsoever.

When news of the Stamp Act's repeal reached the North American colonies, there was general rejoicing. The taverns were crowded with men drinking toasts to their victory; in some cities balls were held; and almost everywhere fireworks were set off, bells were rung, drums were beaten, houses were lighted up, and cannons were fired.

By a strange coincidence, one of the few men who did not enjoy the celebration was John Adams, who had followed the career of the Stamp Act so closely. He confided gloomily to his diary: "A duller day than last Monday, when the province was in a rapture for the repeal of the Stamp Act, I do not remember to have passed. My wife, who had long depended on going to Boston, and my little babe were both very ill of a whooping cough. Myself under obligation to attend the Superior Court at Plymouth the next day, and therefore unable to go to Boston, and the town of Braintree insensible to the common joy."

So great was the feeling of relief and rejoicing among the colonists that most of them failed to understand the full meaning of the Declaratory Act. To them, the repeal of the Stamp Act meant that the English had accepted the colonists' right to levy their own taxes. The declaration that Parliament had power to make laws binding the colonies "in all cases whatsoever" meant to the colonists all cases except taxation.

English people, on the other hand, understood Parliament's

Cartoon published in London after the repeal of the Stamp Act. The British ministers bear the Stamp Act in a coffin to its grave, while ships wait, ready to resume trade with America. (Library of Congress)

power to make laws binding the colonies "in all cases whatsoever" to mean exactly what it said — the case of taxation included.

So, although neither side perhaps fully realized it, nothing had been settled. True, the Stamp Act had been repealed, but there remained a difference of opinion between England and the colonies on taxation and the colonists' rights. The whole question was bound to come up again in the future.

For now, however, it seemed to most people that the dispute was over. Trade with Britain began again, and many of the stamp distributors were allowed to take up their old occupations. Life in the colonies was once more quiet and peaceful.

[56]

The Effects of the Stamp Act

But while the colonies seemed to go back to their former peaceful ways, nothing would ever be the same again.

The colonists had discovered their power. From that time on, they would not hold the royal governors in quite so much respect. The Sons of Liberty had proved what organized resistance could do to British authority. People remembered the terror-stricken stamp distributors. Forgetting the part the British merchants had played, colonial agitators claimed full credit for the repeal of the Stamp Act.

More importantly, the Stamp Act trouble had shown the colonies that they could act in union. Never before had they done this; there had always been rivalries and jealousies among them. But during the tax crisis they had worked together to hold a Stamp Act Congress, to stop trade with England in many ports, and to prevent use of the stamps. The advantages of union were not forgotten. From 1765 on, in moments of difficulty with Great Britain, the colonies took united action.

But perhaps most important of all, the people of the colonies had been aroused. The rights they had taken for granted had been called into question and they had been forced to think about their position as colonists. After 1765, they continued to think and to be more watchful of their rights and liberties. As John Adams said, in speaking of the Stamp Act: "The people, even to the lowest ranks, have become more attentive to their liberties, more inquisitive about them, and more determined to defend them, than they have ever before known or had occasion to be." From then on, the colonists were quick to see tyranny in British acts.

During the trouble about the Stamp Act, many questions had been raised about colonial rights and liberties, and much had been spoken and written in answer in the colonial assemblies and elsewhere in the colonies. After 1765, these declarations of colonial liberties formed a set of principles behind which the colonists remained firm when they felt that their rights were imperiled. The Stamp Act had helped the colonists understand who they were and where they stood. Their belief in their rights and liberties, first clearly defined at the time of the Stamp Act, led them ten years later into the American Revolution.

Selected Bibliography

These works have been especially helpful in the writing of this book.

Adams, John. *The Works of John Adams, with a Life of the Author, Notes, and Illustrations by his Grandson, Charles Francis Adams.* Vol. 2. Boston: Charles C. Little and James Brown, 1850.

Anderson, George P. "Ebenezer Mackintosh, Stamp Act Rioter." Colonial Society of Massachusetts. *Transactions,* 26 (1927).

Braeman, John, *The Road to Independence: A Documentary History of the Causes of the American Revolution, 1763–1776.* New York: G. P. Putnam's Sons, 1963.

Hutchinson, Thomas. *The History of the Colony and Province of Massachusetts Bay.* Vol. 3. Edited by Lawrence Shaw Mayo. Cambridge, Massachusetts: Harvard University Press, 1936.

Knollenberg, Bernhard. *Origins of the American Revolution: 1759–1766.* Rev. ed. New York: The Macmillan Company, 1960.

Miller, John C. *Origins of the American Revolution.* Stanford, California: Stanford University Press, 1959.

Morgan, Edmund S. and Helen M. *The Stamp Act Crisis: Prologue to Revolution.* Chapel Hill: University of North Carolina Press, 1953.

Oliver, Peter. *Origin and Progress of the American Rebellion: a Tory View.* Edited by Douglass Adair and John A. Schulz. Stanford, California: Stanford University Press, 1961.

Index